Shut Up, Shut Up Devil

We Have the Authority to Put Satan to Shame by Just One Name—JESUS. God has Given Us through Jesus's Name to Conquer all the Tests.

THANDIWE RACHEL MPOMELA

WESTBOW
PRESS®
A DIVISION OF THOMAS NELSON
& ZONDERVAN

WestBow Press books may be ordered through booksellers or by contacting:

WestBow Press
A Division of Thomas Nelson & Zondervan
1663 Liberty Drive
Bloomington, IN 47403
www.westbowpress.com
1 (866) 928-1240

ISBN: 978-1-5127-1062-5 (sc)

Library of Congress Control Number: 2015914136

Print information available on the last page.

WestBow Press rev. date: 09/11/2015

CONTENTS

ACKNOWLEDGEMENTS

I am highly blessed and honoured to be given the opportunity and blessings to write about one of the Greatest Man of God Apostle Professor Jeremiah Makananisa. Whoever read this book because this is the message direct from God, will be blessed in Jesus name.

- To all the people who bought my books
  1. I Was Left With an Inch to Go down and
  2. If Shoes Are Tight, Untie the Shoelace, Change the Size or Give the Needy.

- We thank God for this work Wow!! What a great combination between Apostle J. Makananisa the Man of God with so much Power and Revelation and the Author Thandiwe Rachel Mpomela who put it into book form. You can't read this book without being touched by the word it shows us Thandiwe was born to do this; she has a way with words she is a blessing to the Kingdom of God.

  Pastor C.S.Mahlangu, South Africa

- I am so excited and inspired by her books. God bless her abundantly.

  Boniwe Hazel Nthaudi.

- I'm still saying to this day, I never thought you had such writing skills. At first I was a bit reluctant to get myself those copies, but after reading the first book........one could tell that this is the beginning of good things. An Author should be able to reach through readers mind sets. I was indeed amazed at the spiritual maturity of the author. If God says yes no one can say no. "Whoever thought that one day we would be reading your books this is quite an achievement.........I'm actually proud to be amongst the people celebrating your achievement!!!!!!! Just wish nothing but the best for you".

  Mbali Ntombela, Mahikeng

- Her books has inspired me on my relationships, its either with my family or close friends. It taught me how to face challenges in real life. The author reminds us not to forget who we are and where we come from. I personally met her, she is awesome, good and very humble and she gives you the best advice and always reminding you to read the word of God.

Tina, Rustenburg

- The books are very enlightening and inspiring, I believe she is finishing another book as I can't wait longer".

Katlego Josly Molefe, North West

ABOUT THE BOOK

This book was written from the sermons of Apostle Jerry Makananisa. His sermons and preaching's are powerful and are inspiring that's why I was inspired to put it in writing to share with the whole world the Grace that is upon his life and in Ministry.

When you come to Charis Missionary Church the Book of Acts in the bible comes alive by signs and wonders and miracles. All manner of diseases and broken bodies are being healed. This Ministry was started in Thembisa in 1999 September 19 with just a hand full of members in Thembisa Zone 10 and by the Grace of God the church grew tremendously and relocated to Winnie-Mandela Park Zone 5 to date.

The anointing is too much; many people receive Prophecy, Healing and Deliverance and Blessings. **Apostle Professor Jerry Makananisa** also plants churches all over the world (e.g. UK-London, Italy-Barcelona, Sweden, Nigeria, Kenya, DRC and many more) and give impartation to Pastors from other denomination. He feed the poor and the hungry; He is one of the great God's generals. He was raised by God for the times such as these and many people are coming from all over the world to hear a word from God. Apostle Makananisa is a great Father of a great family. His wife **Prophetess Dr. Eunice Makananisa** is a great worshipper.

My aim is to share the great light that is coming out of South of Africa so that there'll be awareness of these Great men of God worldwide. No one comes into contact with him (Apostle Jerry Makananisa) that is not touched by the Grace and Love that oozes out of God, He is so humbled……………………..

Prayer by Apostle Jerry Makananisa:
My Jesus!
Holy Father!
I Am Going To Do Your Will
And
I Want to See Your Will in My Life.
I Am Receiving Your Will
And
I Will Never Suffer Again in Jesus Mighty Name.
AMEN!!!!!!!!

To

_____

From

_____

This book is dedication to the Glory of God,
And to all Christians around the Globe
Who support Man of God without fear
To
Bring down
The
Work of a devil,
Alerting children of God
That
Nothing is impossible with our Almighty God.

If we repent 100% to Christ without looking back,
God is giving us a guarantee
To
live a happy life, stress free, debt free, no diseases
And Eternal life.

ABOUT JERRY MAKANANISA

It is very hard to imagine the world without Prophets or Pastors. A world without the father, the healer, the guider and the world without a place whereby you could just walk into a church like Charis Missionary Church and feel safe, feel home, heeled and welcomed by everyone with a warm hearts full of Gospel.

Apostle Jerry Makananisa is one in a million Prophet who takes or spend most of his time doing God's work. He has everything that anyone can dream of but he does not even care about those material things because he knows it's his blessings and more things are comings.

Imagine all those fancy cars, beautiful houses and cash that can make him to travel or tour the continent but just because he knows where he comes from, where God is taking him, Apostle Makananisa and his wife Pastor Eunice Makananisa are so relaxed in the house of God and they enjoy doing the work of God together every second throughout the year.

Apostle Makananisa keeps on blessings every member of Charis, Christians watching Charis TV, Charis partners, Thembisa residents who are disadvantaged but not only Thembisa he blesses everyone around the world, He assist Pastors, individuals around the world with accommodation, food, clothes, cars etc.

If God can raise Prophets, Pastors like Apostle Makananisa the world will be saved.

Let us all join hands and support him in any way we can to make sure Charis Missionary Church expand with powerful Prophets and Pastors and cover the seven continents. He will live to be our Spiritual father or Grandfather in the name of our father, our God Almighty in Jesus Mighty name.

Prophets like Apostle Jerry Makananisa are very few and we Christians must join together to support them. He is married and blessed with kids.

Prophetess Eunice Makananisa is indeed a mother of all nations; she gave her heart to serve God and made sure all her children follow their steps. Both Mama and Papa raised Prophets, singers, leaders from their home. With their background they agreed and joined their heart to bless Christians with cars, houses, connections, employments, healthy life and free from all chronically diseases etc.

Some came with fruit of the womb problem and Apostle blessed them with kids and some came with testimonies holding kids on their hands including those who were told by professional Doctors that they are barren but by His anointing he proved Satan wrong by showing Satan that if God says Yes no one can say no.

There are very few women out there educated like Eunice Makananisa who support their husband in every angle. Doctor Makananisa Eunice and Professor Makananisa Jerry out ruled their professional titles and enjoy the ones given to them by God (Apostle and Pastor). The two are united and spend most of their time together in the house of God (Thembisa) and when they are home in one of the Suburbs around Johannesburg they join together with their children to sing or practice gospel songs. If one needs to understand the meaning of multi task please come to Makananisa family and you will get all the answers that can change you to become a useful Christian, living and enjoying life without checking time or planning for other things that are not Godley.

I personally thank God For the Makananisa Family.

Apostle Jerry Makananisa loves what he's doing and he always want to make sure you leave Charis Missionary Church healed, blessed. He is a reliable Prophet. Charis visitors know how this great man of god takes time during one on one session and he is always in church seven days a week. He does not believe in serving God part time especially when you are called. Remember he is a Professor by profession and he can get any job anywhere if he wants to but he know and believes in the anointing that he carry.

Apostle Jerry Makananisa taught us so many things like how to differentiate between Suffering and when God is about to raise you. He stressed the fact that when you have a calling you have to pay the price, you can loose your own family all turned against you, You can loose your friend, your job, your kids, your wealth. You can be hated by those around you. If you have the spiritual eye and ears you will accept your situation knowing its temporary and start by thanking God for all the blessing coming your way. And when you are lonely, hated and broke you can be used by God easily and your enemies will start to notice your God.

Apostle always advices those Pastors with ministries not to worry for members who left their church because God is about to shock them, by doing something and bringing people who will bless their ministries ten times. Apostle said one lost member is replaced by one thousand members. And he asked them not to curse them but bless everyone who left their ministries and not to allow them to come back to their ministries.

Apostle said we all have spirit of discernment that can guide and lead you if we know the signs. Without Spirit of discernment you are lost and possibilities of you falling in wrong hands, ministries, and fake prophets is very high. You will believe everything that you are told or see with your naked eyes.

We Christians we must ask him to teach us how to pray just like Jesus taught his disciples in Luke 11:1. **"One of His Disciples said to him, Lord, teach us to pray".**

The answer to prayer is part of prayer which glorifies God. You cannot flourish in God without Jesus anointing because his anointing does not work on the unfaithful or the wicked.

YOU ARE A WONDER

These words can be said to a person one admires and we praise them for who they are and the things they do, this is an ongoing praise for those who are doing it according to God's will. Apostle said there is something that he saw which is beyond doubt affecting each and every one of us in this point in time. It is true that prayer counts but even sin counts. We can pray as much as we can but if we keep on doing the same things that we know they are not holy we are wasting our moment.

We Christians should avoid living like pigs because they do as they please. (Isa_66:3).

I believe that if we keep on doing as we please is like leaving the steering of the vehicle while driving and by doing that we can get the accident or fall into a trap, not only the driver but those who are with him in the vehicle and those in front of your car or driving behind you. So every action has its own results whether big or small.

What does it mean getting an accident as a Christian and affecting those who are around you? Do check your character as a Christian and the speed you are driving in your spiritual life.

Never ever go to church to fool around or to please anyone or show off, says Apostle Jerry Makananisa in one his church services. He said we came alone and whatever we do or say we shouldn't mind the person sitting next to you in church. There is no community of property in church whether you go together in groups does not mean God will treat you the same. Everyone has his/her own cross to carry and if e keep on doing wrong things is the more we open doors for any evil spirits to enter our life's. We must all remember that our body is the body of Christ and we need to keep it clean at all times.

Miracles come to those people who don't care about the outside world when they are in the house of God, They don't care what the clothes they are wearing or how good or bad they sing. These people they just connect with God and allow Him to use them after all "LE TLAILA LE TLAILELA MORENENG".

You are born alone and you will die alone. You came alone in this world and you will leave this world alone

Why Christians are not progressing

He said many of Christians are not moving forward because they are living a double life, being a Christian on Sundays but immediately when they leave the house of God they change into being something else. We should not be Christian only in the house of the Lord and continue to live a Sinful life when we are outside the church. God opposes the proud but gives grace to the humble. When we leave the house of God we must not change into being something else like living a Christianity and Sinning outside the church. Christian attains self-worth and esteem by having the right relationship with God. God paid a high price through the blood of his son, Jesus Christ.

Christianity in the Church and you live a sinful life when you are out of church. Satan traps people during December because the month of December is actually a month for Christians to renew their strength of following Christ. When you fail in December, the whole year you will be in the dark. Satan works well in December December is a very dangerous month because everyone is thinking of how and where to spend their holidays and only few choose church but the rest choose Satan's ways.

God is watching us from a distance when no one is watching and when our heart is shattered. God is watching you, God is watching me, God is watching us from January to December even before we were born God knew everything about you.

Fornication and Alcoholics cleaning church

The reason why the Church of God doesn't have the Holy Spirit is because we have fornicators (intercourse between two people not married to each other) and drunkards cleaning the Church and there is no one to reprimand them. (Revelation 2:14, 20)

When Christians have the tendency to come late to church but going to school or work they make sure they arrive early to safe their employment where they work or to avoid their employer to deduct their salary or wage, or arrive early at school just to be on the good books of school teacher or avoiding to be sent back home until the school decides the student punishment. You go to school the teacher would beat you not to come late but now in the Church there is no reprimanding and you do all that you want. There is no commandment in the Bible that says, "Thou shall not be late to church "every one claiming to be a Christian must check him/herself. Sometimes it's just a matter of changing those habits to be more aware of time.

Some has a habit of late coming and they are not even concerned about the time or vice versa some come very early because they want to be noticed or seen on TV not because they are here to pray. And most of front sitters don't pay tithe, when it comes to offerings they are the last ones to come in front.

Sitting in front does not guarantee you as a Christian a place in heaven. As with all things, God looks at the heart, "for the lord does not see as man sees; for man looks at the outward appearance, but the lord looks at the heart" (1 Samuel 16:7)

Love, Material and your Relationship with God

If your love is based in materials and you want to capture many things by one month and you forget the whole year. Some of the things you own end up owning you love them whole heartedly forgetting how you got them. Many of you start knowing there is God after losing everything they owned. Many of you don't know that Satan wants to kill you.

If your fellowship with the Lord is based on money and materials you won't succeed because all these things must die and love must remain. The needs that we cry or die to satisfy them can only be accomplished when you accepted Jesus in your heart, and they will last forever. Whatever you earn or acquire by cheating or robbing others won't last forever. When other people are falling because of sin, you will enjoy your walk with Christ.

A real man or woman will fall in love with your words, not your looks since looks can deceive you. Many people are dying because of the wrong choices they made. Because of the partners they chose based on their looks and material.

Husband, Wives, Christians, Check your Character

Sin is our enemy says Apostle Makananisa and he asked the congregation and those watching on the screen to verify themselves, To check their Character. Many married couples will fight but to you who are reading and this and believe in God Almighty, it will never come to pass. Husband and wife, don't fight each other. Have peace that will direct you to your joy and enjoy this Christmas. You will enjoy this Christmas. Devil wants to frustrate you and mix you up. We must not just take a journey, we have to sit down with our families and pray. We have to be very much careful and avoid sinning.

According to God's word, when you become a Christian a part of your new creation is the development of new attitudes.

We somehow face some challenges that are there to shake our faith. When you face a challenge, one must tell her/himself that God is still in control. Persecution is there because of the word of God. The moment you have God's word, it will make you produce what you want in life. When we live in Sin, Satan can trap us in so many things.

Sin Our Number One Enemy and Satan is using it because he does not have a brain, Satan is brainless.

Just check only one sin that is haunting you. Some says when they are angry they lose all the brakes; some can kill some use wrong words.

We must learn to chose words wisely and deal with self if we want to see the kingdom of God. The bible says we are all called but only few are chosen.

For you to know if you fit to be a Faithful Christians there are things that you need to check like your character and other things that can classify you as a Christian.

"5 But you know that he appeared so that he might take away our sins. And in him is no sin. 6 No one who lives in him keeps on sinning. No one who continues to sin has either seen him or known him." 1 John 3:5-6 (TNIV)

From the above Scriptures, Apostle Makananisa said we will realise that Sin is our number one enemy and maybe this is why Jesus never taught us to fight our enemies because He manifested His appearance to Deal with Sin. He continued saying when Jesus appeared, it was to fight Sin and to take it away. He who Sins, has never seen Jesus or known Him this means Sin separates us with Him and many of us are praying asking God why things are not happening not checking our character. He advised everyone to look at their Life. Sin is there to nullify your knowledge of Christ, to remove that understanding out of us and also to prove all of us bluntly that we do not know Him (Christ).

Sin is our biggest enemy, opponent in our choices; it makes us not to know the One we think we know. Satan doesn't mind, he does not care to those who are just going to Church, Sunday faces, he minds about those who ask forgiveness from their Sins because by them doing that he thinks he lost power over your life. You can attend church daily but if you have that secret that you are hiding he knows you are dishonest so it qualifies you to be his candidate and they will keep on praying letting pastors know that some of their church members are snakes.

Sin makes us to be an enemy of Jesus Christ, if Jesus was manifested to take sin away and we keep on sinning; automatically Jesus was manifested to take us away. The more we sin, the more we become sin.

The meaning of Sin means, SATAN.

The moment we do wrong against God our creator, we open doors for Satan to enter. If we tell lies or keep any deadly secrets he enters into our lives very easily. Christians can sin by mistake but confessing it is to close doors for Satan to enter. The moment you know you did wrong you better apologise fast before the sun set so that Satan cannot come and steal your Glory.

The communion was advised to seriously take track of their lives. And also to check their lives daily starting from now and see if whether Satan is in your live or not, to check if you are perfectly honest including the tithes and offerings they are paying.

We must be aware that the moment Satan is in your life, you are defined as sin.

"⁷ If you do what is right, will you not be accepted? But if you do not do what is right, sin is crouching at your door; it desires to have you, but you must rule over it." **Genesis 4:7** *(TNIV)*

Cain was told that if he didn't do well, sin was at his door and being told that he is given the opportunity to ask for forgiveness. We all need to understand that when you don't do right you allow sin to come to you.

"¹ Now the serpent was craftier than any of the wild animals the LORD God had made. He said to the woman, "Did God really say, 'You must not eat from any tree in the garden'?" **Genesis 3:1** *(TNIV)*

Disobedience comes when you begin to listen to Satan. By disobedience you automatically open a door to communicate with Satan. Adam and Eve were to reject Satan but they gave him an opportunity to explain or to deceive them.

The more you try to explain to Satan, he will manipulate you. Your Christian life must not be a life of explaining but you must live it in accordance with the word of God.

Satan took advantage and told Eve that God was lying. Whenever you sin against God, you disobey Him and you listen to Satan. Check your character because what you talk nullifies your prayer.

The Book of Isaiah says that your sins separate you with the hand of God. God was saying that it is not that His far, the problem is our sins (see Isaiah 59:1-2).

Everyone can seem to be Holy in church, but there is a spot where Satan finds you. Our God is a God of secret. He said when you pray you must close the door and pray, unfortunately when many of you pray, when God looks at your closets He finds you with Satan.

A Christian needs to pray a prayer of change. Change and change forever not temporary because the moment you say you accepted Jesus or you changed Satan will always come tease you and reminds you of all the things you are missing.

When you start by going to church your friends will start by calling you names. When you pay Tithes according to God's will they will bring more responsibilities or problems and make you choose between paying tithes or attending to their problems.

They will make you feel you are wasting money and make you feel useless and irresponsible.

This is the time now whereby your Faith will be tested, your honestly will be tested your character will be tested. So be Wise and do the right thing that will last you forever.

Plant the fruits that will be there forever. If ever your friends and relatives decides to leave you because you are not doing what pleases them Apostle said we should not worry because wrong friends, wrongs relatives will go.

Just like dry tree leaves they will fall down and the new ones will grow even if it takes time to show but we must be happy that Jesus removes dirty leaves out of our lives.

You can be fired from your employment, don't worry that was the erroneous leaf, you might be divorced don't be troubled that was the erroneous leaf.

Your family can reject you but don't be troubled because they are the erroneous leaf and God will create new family, better husband, better wife, job replacing the ones who left you thinking you wont survive without them but they Forgot the One and Only thing, God is watching you from a distance and he can allow certain things to happen in your life like challenges so that He can use you.

Wao!! Wao!! I love my God, He is the God of wonders and he always makes a way where there is no way.

"¹⁷ So then, if you know the good you ought to do and don't do it, you sin." **James 4:17** (TNIV)

Everyone who knows the difference between right and wrong and know how to avoid Satan's voice in any how they will be sin free.

We must all be aware that Satan is always watching us like eagle to do wrong so that he can steal our glory. We must never copy any one's life style because you end up competing for the things that you do not know. If we start by living our own life be you not someone else we will definitely see the Glory of God in us.

Sometimes copying other people's style we end up copying wrong things that will lead us to open doors for Satan and he will take what belongs to us.

We must live right and follow Jesus and always be quick to apologise to shame devil. Don't be afraid to let the Devil know how stupid he is. Just say "SHUT UP DEVIL".

Jesus is busy preparing the table in front of your enemies and you will dominate, you will overtake them, you'll take back your position and you will start enjoying the things that you're enemies, your relatives, your neighbours do not have.

As a believer you can possess the things that you did not struggle to get or pay for them.

How Sin begins:

"¹⁷ For the sinful nature desires what is contrary to the Spirit, and the Spirit what is contrary to the sinful nature. They are in conflict with each other, so that you are not to do whatever you want." **Galatians 5:17** *(TNIV)*

The reason why you start sinning shows that there is a battle, the flesh against your spirit. There is a battle when the flesh becomes stronger, it over powers your soul but if your soul is having the word of God and is living on that word, that word will give your soul strength and the flesh will be weak. When you sin you sin against your soul and when you are overpowering sin you live for your soul.

Check your character for it will show you where you have overcome. If you are sinning, automatically it means the flesh is dominating.

Whoever dominates in you rules your life.

We need to be very careful, whoever dominates in you rules and is the one to affect you Positively or Negatively. The reason why many won't go to heaven is because their souls are already detained in hell and their flesh is just living here on earth. There are some people who find themselves sleeping whenever they open the Bible; this is because the flesh is dominating.

When your soul is dominated with the righteousness of God, when you pray you will see results. Many of us are just doing things and not checking if we are in flesh or in Spirit. If you don't check, whatever you do might seem right to you but not before God.

Results of sin:

"15 Then, after desire has conceived, it gives birth to sin; and sin, when it is full-grown, gives birth to death." **James 1:15** (TNIV)

Sin brings Death. Sin is not Good, It is our Enemy.

"23 for all have sinned and fall short of the glory of God," **Romans 3:23** (TNIV)

Apostle said sin makes us to run short of the Glory of God; as a Christian you won't manifest in your fullness.

We are supposed to manifest like Jesus. If we fall short of His Glory, there won't be any difference in our present time and the future. If we are working in small position in small companies we must get a position that shows we are serving the living God.

As Christians we cannot stay in stagnation. If we are staying in small houses we need to shift to better houses, those in a sharks must move to mansions, those in locations must move to suburbs. Christians are not born to be poor or sick. We are the sons and daughters of all the riches in the world as Satan owns Zero.

The righteous ones must get what satan stole from tem, their positions and reach their destiny without fail. If they want luxury cars they must claim them and believe they already have them and by just doing that the moment they enter the garage they will get their heart desire.

They must be blessed with new houses and they must at least try to avoid second hand cars and moving in other people's houses. You are not called for other's rejects since the wealth and riches of the world belong to you if you believe. They must learn to build their own houses and avoid by all means houses that they do not know their foundations.

The Glory of God might not be visible to you now but it is bound to be. People must look at you and praise your God because of the life you are living, the things you have especially those who thought or believed you will never have some things; those rated you zero because they think they know your History (etc Geography or Biology).

As the Bible says you are the head and not the tail, you are supposed to be above and if you are above, everyone must see you, they must see us.

Apostle said we must shine our shine and because of this we will rise above.

Every door will be open and our enemies will start to bless us.

When John saw the Glory in Jesus, he could not be silenced.

The disciples of John heard John say,

"The lamb of God that took the sins of the whole world". There was Glory to make John utter the greatness in Jesus.

Overcome Sin to your Glory you must question yourself What is it that is stealing that Glory?

You must honour and splendour at all the times. Sin no more.

Rom 8:17 -18 "Since we are his children, we will possess the blessings he keeps for his people, and we will also possess with Christ what God has kept for him; for if we share Christ's suffering, we will also share his glory. I consider that what we suffer at this present time cannot be compared at all with the glory that is going to be revealed to us.

Sin that rules you steals the Glory of God in your life. Paul was telling the Romans, when sin dominates in you, you want to do certain things but you can't do them. Sin has its own dimension of life; it is there to disarray you, to confuse you to take your focus in wrong direction.

You can change your direction because of sin. Many thought they were going up or they are on top of the world and expecting to reach to another higher level but the moment sin entered their thought, their life, Satan began to rule their life. Don't allow sin to take over. Sin brings its own direction and plans.

The Bible tells us that we have been predestined (see Ephesians 1:5), meaning all things have been placed before us but sin will come to take us off that road which leads to our destiny. Many people are asking why things are not working out well for them; ***Don't look at Those Things, Look at Yourself and Confess Your Sins. GOD will take you there.***

"Sin wants you to take short cuts to your blessings. Sin will always draw a line of going to your destiny; when sin is at work it delays everything". *Apostle Jerry Makananisa was told this revelation*: all the things that you are supposed to have are there, there is nothing new under the Sun. You start your road to your destiny and in front of your there is your heart desire according to the plan of God but the moment you sin, Satan misdirects you. Your heart desires are still there but you have taken a wrong path.

God will take you back after repentance, but the moment he does you sin again because of the blessings. Your direction will always mislead you not to receive your full blessings.

If you live right, any delay serves a purpose and you won't miss your blessings. When you are on the right pathway, you take all that belongs to you all for the Glory of God.

The delay of the righteous is meant for God's best time for the salvation of those around you. Don't allow Satan to condemn you.

You are on the right track; when you are delayed just rejoice because you will never miss your blessings.

It may look tough but if you are not in sin you are on the right track and when you are on the right track you will hear people speaking, but don't look unto those persecutions, look unto all which lies ahead of you.

Don't look on the side; carry on with your head held high. When you hear them talk, they invite you to sin. When you answer a fool, you become a fool.

People Can Lie About You; They Can Gossip About You And Also Trouble You but You can't BE Stopped.

Don't sin against God because of your situations, don't worry; just look unto where you are going.

When Jesus had an encounter with His accusers, He could not mind what they were say to Him because many of them where there to make him sin.

Do you know that trying to prove your righteousness to your accusers is sin?

"8 If we claim to be without sin, we deceive ourselves and the truth is not in us. 9 If we confess our sins, he is faithful and just and will forgive us our sins and purify us from all unrighteousness." **1 John 1:8-9** *(TNIV)*

This verse carries a guarantee of our forgiveness says Apostle. It says nothing about time.

You receive the righteousness of God now, you pray now and something will happen now.

What is it that is difficult for you to stop doing? You can confess your sins and He is faithful and just to forgive your sins. He is always ready to hear you say *sorry*.

Judge yourself before you are judged. Sin is our enemy. We preach it because it is our enemy working to separate us from the one who has died for us.

CONFIDENCE IN THE FLESH AND DENYING CHRIST

This is one of the messages from Apostle Jerry Makananisa's service saying this is a warning to Christians.

"35 But Peter declared, "Even if I have to die with you, I will never disown you." And all the other disciples said the same. 75 Then Peter remembered the word Jesus had spoken: "Before the rooster crows, you will disown me three times." And he went outside and wept bitterly" **Matthew 26:35, 75** *(TNIV)*

Many of us think that we are walking with the Lord not knowing that we have denied Him. Denying Christ is as good as having Confidence in the Flesh.

You know who you are in the Flesh and you rely in your own abilities. If you read about Peter you will realise that he was having Confidence in his own Flesh. He told Jesus that he was ready to die with Him. Many of us are so Confident in our own Flesh that we even speak statements that will be required tomorrow and therefore we end up changing our decisions.

Many of you agree with God when things are looking good but when things are bad we disagree with Him. You will see Peter trying to advise Jesus telling Him that he has a level that makes him better than the other disciples.

You can question why Peter said all that he said to Jesus.

Remember that Peter gave up his profession and followed Jesus just like Apostle Jerry Makananisa (Professor Makananisa) and his beautiful and intelligent wife Pastor Eunice Makananisa (Doctor Makananisa). The initial step he took made him feel like he will always stand. This is a challenge to us. In verse 75 you could see Peter remembering the words of Jesus.

Peter was supposed to question Jesus that why He had said that he would deny Him because he needed to overcome this trial. Peter took it to himself; he had Confidence in his initial decision.

The Bible states that Peter left the presence of Jesus after Jesus had told him that he had failed the statement he had initially said of dying with Jesus. Peter recognised his failure as the bible states that he didn't cry historically but bitterly.

You become blessed when you recognise where you fall or fail. Many of us try to smile everyday showing our Confidence in the Flesh but spiritually we are defeated. The reason why many are sick is because we pose to be big where else we have fallen. Peter cried bitterly meaning he cried that everyone saw it. He cried until that those who were around him could see that something was wrong.

Do you know that when you want to overcome having Confidence in your Flesh, you overcome it by facing it yourself? You become yourself when you approach Jesus with your weaknesses as well as your strengths and He will teach you how you are to overcome.

The reason why we fail is because we are hypocrites. We come in the image of other people where else we are not living outlives.

"¹⁷Join together in following my example, brothers and sisters, and just as you have us as a model, keep your eyes on those who live as we do. ¹⁸For, as I have often told you before and now tell you again even with tears, many live as enemies of the cross of Christ.

¹⁹Their destiny is destruction, their god is their stomach, and their glory is in their shame. Their mind is set on earthly things. ²⁰But our citizenship is in heaven. And we eagerly await a Savior from there, the Lord Jesus Christ," **Philippians 3:17-20** *(TNIV)*

If you mind about your stomach better than your Spiritual life then you are already destructed; you don't have a destiny or a vision. You need to know that in whatever you do God marks.

"³For it is we who are the circumcision, we who serve God by his Spirit, who boast in Christ Jesus, and who put no confidence in the flesh— ⁴though I myself have reasons for such confidence. If others think they have reasons to put confidence in the flesh, I have more: ⁵circumcised on the eighth day, of the people of Israel, of the tribe of Benjamin, a Hebrew of Hebrews; in regard to the law, a Pharisee". **Philippians 3:3-5***(TNIV)*

Paul said before he preaches he deals with his Flesh. He was ready to destroy his flesh for Christ. In whatever you do God marks. I love David when he said that his Confidence lied in the Lord. He could not do anything unless he consulted God. Many of us consult God only when it is tough. We consider only all that make us better.

"**16**They claim to know God, but by their actions they deny him. They are detestable, disobedient and unfit for doing anything good." **Titus 1:16** (TNIV),

If you claim to know God but deny Him, you are unfit for every good work. You need to cut everyone around you. It is of useless to gain the whole world while your soul is dying. He who does not have Confidence in the Flesh judges himself before he is judged. Don't try to know God when you are denying Him. You are becoming unfit for every good work.

Stages of a Christian's life

There are three stages of a Christian's Life and the first stage is called the Preparation stage:

When God prepares you, you face too much Temptation and many blessings will come in a wrong way. When God is preparing you; there will be a lot of disconnecting rather than connection. For you to stand before God and become righteous you need to pass this stage.

In this stage Grace will appear on you but many of us fail and that is why we have people whose things seem to be promising but go back to zero; it is not failure, it is Preparation. Don't cry to come out of this stage because a blessing that will come will come to rob you. This stage is like a root that needs to go deep down. When God is preparing you, know that your root will be expanding. Don't worry about showing or shooting up.

You will bear fruits when it is not a season of bearing fruits. The problem is people want to shoot out before time and because of this anxiety, when they face calamities they fall away.

Be deep-rooted so that you may be established, you may be recognised and acknowledged; Confidence in the Flesh is very dangerous. When you don't have pain that does not mean you are not ill. Many of you find that you are ill only when you feel pain and this will take the direction of your prayers.

You don't need to be beautiful or handsome to enjoy life; you need to be under the umbrella of Jesus Christ. Don't look at your appearance or experience.

"17 But, dear friends, remember what the apostles of our Lord Jesus Christ foretold. 18 They said to you, "In the last times there will be scoffers who will follow their own ungodly desires."

19 These are the people who divide you, who follow mere natural instincts and do not have the Spirit.

20 But you, dear friends, by building yourselves up in your most holy faith and praying in the Holy Spirit, 21 keep yourselves in God's love as you wait for the mercy of our Lord Jesus Christ to bring you to eternal life." **Jude 1:17-21** *(TNIV)*

Build yourself on Holy faith and don't try to imitate anyone. Don't try to be in competition with anyone; Compete yourself with yourself.

If you do that you will know that you are not a failure. Remember that you are born and bred by the word of God. Don't look at your CV, if you look at you qualifications you will be having Confidence in the Flesh.

Press forward like Paul and take your blessings. Get out of your dustbin and go to your Mansion.

HEARING GOD'WORD

The problem we have today is not because the word of God is not being preached. Our problem is hearing. Many of us don't know that Jesus spoke several times about Hearing.

"¹¹ As Scripture says, "Anyone who believes in him will never be put to shame." ¹² For there is no difference between Jew and Gentile— the same Lord is Lord of all and richly blesses all who call on him, ¹³ for, "Everyone who calls on the name of the Lord will be saved." **Romans 10:11-13** *(TNIV)*

If you can hear the word of God you will realise that there must be a preacher whom is sent. If the preacher is sent then there will be faith and if there is faith somebody must get it by hearing.

The preacher must preach and after hearing you will be able to call upon God.

This shows that there is no base of calling someone you have not heard about. Our answers are based on our hearing because you cannot just call not expecting results. Many of us don't know that our base is by hearing.

¹⁴ How, then, can they call on the one they have not believed in? And how can they believe in the one of whom they have not heard? And how can they hear without someone preaching to them?

¹⁵ And how can anyone preach unless they are sent? As it is written: "How beautiful are the feet of those who bring good news!"

¹⁷ Consequently, faith comes from hearing the message, and the message is heard through the word about Christ." **Romans 10:11-13** *(TNIV)*

When you are hearing, obedience comes and this shows your belief and your belief brings out your life style. Many of us are calling upon the Lord but we don't believe according to obedience.

Many say they are hearing but their life styles are not showing. If we are truly hearing; when we call something must happen.

The problem is not that you are not calling but the problem is that you are not hearing.

"27 My sheep listen to my voice; I know them, and they follow me. **John 10:27** *(TNIV)*

Your destiny has been determined by your hearing. You cannot follow Jesus unless your hear Him. Where you are is determined by your hearing.

If you hear that God is with you, you will realise that no can stop you. People who can't hear have limitations in what they believe. If you are following God you are bound to be unlimited.

He who guides you is there when you are hearing and is not limited. Your hearing is limited.

Hearing is so important. When was the last time you hear God. So people are busy with remedies where else they can't follow instructions. The Bible says we must listen to instructions.

"5 It is better to heed the rebuke of a wise person than to listen to the song of fools." **Ecclesiastes 7:5** (TNIV)

Somebody can just listen to a song and whilst God will be trying to warn you but not hearing. Changes come when you hear God.

You can still hear songs of fools who say there is no God but change will only come when you begin to hear God.

We can make many sacrifices which are not needed called abominations. If you can't hear and resent to prayer, your prayer becomes wasted.

Many can still pray because everyone can talk but few can obey what they are hearing. It is not easy to hear because your hearing is not an issue of hearing sound but it must affect your responsibility.

God is speaking to most of you but you are not responding. Even what you are hearing does not affect you to respond towards where God is directing you.

There are some people now God is ready to destroy because they don't mind about what God is saying. Your prayer can be wasted though you pray. Check your hearing before you do anything.

"14 The farmer sows the word. 15 Some people are like seed along the path, where the word is sown. As soon as they hear it, Satan comes and takes away the word that was sown in them.

[16] Others, like seed sown on rocky places, hear the word and at once receive it with joy. [17] But since they have no root, they last only a short time. When trouble or persecution comes because of the word, they quickly fall away. **Mark 4:14-17** *(TNIV)*

Jesus showed the importance of hearing. Jesus showed that those who are on the way side, they hear the word of God but Satan comes. Jesus realised that there are four kinds of people; they can hear but they don't know what happens later.

When you read the last verse of producing fruits, you will understand that hearing responds with your productivity. Your success is determined by your hearing.

When the ground is good and seed is sown into it, it germinates and grows and there will be a harvest. If there is no harvest, question your hearing.

Don't judge people, many times we point at other people.

[18] Still others, like seed sown among thorns, hear the word; [19] but the worries of this life, the deceitfulness of wealth and the desires for other things come in and choke the word, making it unfruitful. [20] Others, like seed sown on good soil, hear the word, accept it, and produce a crop—some thirty, some sixty, some a hundred times what was sown." **Mark 4:18-20** *(TNIV)*

Many of us are trying to solve things that we have started by our own will and we end up asking God to intervention.

We must appreciate the other ways of our God Mighty when he is silent, means he is saying something.

Just like the Teacher or invigilator, during the exam time he keeps quite and collects the exam answer sheet after exams and he will mark them silently and only speaks when he gives out the final marks.

As Christians we must know that when the results come out after our life exams or challenges, our enemies will be shocked.

When you are on the way side you cannot be productive; Sharpen your hearing. Not long I found that many people around us have been deploying in our lives by the devil with missions to come and dilute our faith - our hearing.

They tell you things of no value. If you answer a fool you become a fool and he who fights faith fights God.

Not all people around you are people. You must define them and discern them by hearing.

The Devil might be using them to block you because they talk nonsense and the moment they do, your breakthrough becomes nonsense.

It comes from hearing and not what you can utter; what you can utter makes sense if what you hear is important. I don't want to hear nonsense. Your hearing connects you with the person on the other side.

"15 For this people's hearts have become calloused; they hardly hear with their ears, and they have closed their eyes. Otherwise they might see with their eyes, hear with their ears, understand with their hearts and turn, and I would heal them.'" **Matthew 13:15** *(TNIV)*

This is a very touching verse. This is telling us that our healing is not in the pastor. Many of us can't understand. In Mark 4 I realised that hearing doesn't only bring Satan but also afflictions and sufferings.

Many preach Christianity as an easy pathway to follow. Christianity is a battle ground. The moment you hear and take it, there will be afflictions.

Those afflictions are there to bring testimonies. You can be a poor Christian but it is for a big testimony.

A Christian can still rejoice in suffering knowing the One he/she is serving. Wisdom is the application of knowledge.

Wisdom it is brought by understanding what you can apply to bring results and therefore you will not worry.

Many of us because we lack understanding our ears are dull and there is no adaptation.

Christians must be converted meaning that though they may face things to make them worry, they won't worry as they KNOW the truth.

We must ignore the things that Satan is doing by only concentrating on the good things that our Almighty God is doing or communicating.

If we can realise where He is taking us and where he took us from we will be thankful.

Our friends can still laugh at us but we will see the best things the Lord has set before as we are more than a conquer.

!!!!! If You can Take the Word of God, You are Dangerous to Satan.!!!!!!!!

GOD'S WORD

Satan always loves to destroy the people of God. If Satan wants to break the Family, he brings deception.

If you can realise that you are no longer honest, or faithful you must know that SATAN knocked in your door and you gladly opened the door for him.

Since you are the one who opened the door, you will be the one to make a U-turn and Shut Him UP for your glory.

Pray more, Talk less to avoid demons

"²²Then Judas (not Judas Iscariot) said, "But, Lord, why do you intend to show yourself to us and not to the world?"

²³Jesus replied, "Anyone who loves me will obey my teaching. My Father will love them, and we will come to them and make our home with them.

²⁴Anyone who does not love me will not obey my teaching. These words you hear are not my own; they belong to the Father who sent me." **John 14:22-24** *(TNIV)*

You will realise that the question that was asked by Judas shows that the word of God for us is important.

Judas wanted to know the difference of between them and the world. Judas was asking for a sign of showing them that they will be able see Jesus all the time.

Jesus said that it is only when we keep His word and by doing so, the Father will love us.

Keeping the word is something special, and something challenging; it signifies that we are not breaking the trust between us and Him.

When God gives us the word, we need to perform that word proving that we trust the one who gave us the word.

In *verse 23* Jesus said when you keep the word of God, it makes all three of you (God, Jesus and Yourself) to come and build together.

Apostle said this is a shocking thing - keeping the word. The Father will descend from His chair to dwell within you.

You will be like three-in-one; that's what Jesus was saying. Jesus went forth in *verse 24* that whatever He spoke was not from Him alone but the Father in Him, so when He spoke it was also the Father who spoke.

If you don't keep the word of Jesus you won't keep the word of the Father.

They can fight you not knowing they are fighting God. The word of God says Jesus and the Father will come and do things together in us so when people look at us, they must see our Father and Jesus especially when they attempt to ambush us, they will realise you are invisible.

"¹ In the beginning was the Word, and the Word was with God, and the Word was God.

² He was with God in the beginning. ³ Through him all things were made; without him nothing was made that has been made.

*⁴ In him was life, and that life was the light of all people." **John 1:1-4** (TNIV)*

The above verse talks about Jesus as the word. Jesus said the word He speaks belongs to the Father.

So if now you build with Jesus, when you speak, it will be like the Father or Jesus speaking.

The same Jesus we are talking about is the very same Jesus who has created all things visible.

All things which are visible are not coming any where accept through Jesus Christ.

If Christ is in you, you can create something. If Jesus is the one who created all visible things, now to Him being in you means you can create anything visible.

If Jesus is in you and the Father is in you because you keep the word, and since Jesus is the one who created all things, it means you having kept the word, you will create something.

Jesus created everything by the word. When you speak a word, it shall come to pass.

You are not alone; there is someone greater in you. You have been given authority to create. The words you speak are not yours, you are not alone, and when you say something it will happen as it is.

The problem is that our words puzzle us also. Don't wait for God because He is waiting for you.

Elijah told King Ahab that there would be neither dew nor rain except by his word (see 1 King 17:1).

Many of us need to know that we are not alone and when we speak that's what we will touch.

You are changing and becoming similar to your Creator and whatever you say shall come to pass.

Let us speak big things that we desire and see them happing. Jesus could not waste time.

The disciples of Jesus had a skill of catching fish but there was a particular day they could not catch them.

Jesus told them to lower their nets and that they must not move. Where you are, you don't need to go and borrow money, you don't need to ask for money; you can speak money today and get money today.

You don't need to struggle yourself. Your words are important, they must come to pass.

Stop worrying, you got an answer; when you talk, Apostle Paul said that the word of God is near to you - in your mouth (see Romans 10:8).

Your prosperity is not anywhere in the world but in your words; many of us spend time crying than speaking words of change.

We spend time grumbling. Check what you are speaking all the time, choose words wisely. Stop complaining and pointing fingers at other people.

You can speak something and it will happen, the power of the tongue, you can speak life or death.

Avoid wrong words. Whatever you search from the outside, when you get it won't be enough, but when you get in from the inside you will be satisfied.

*"³ For the ear tests words as the tongue tastes food. ⁴ Let us discern for ourselves what is right; let us learn together what is good." **Job 34:3** (TNIV)*

Your ear that hears the word and brings faith to you makes you to talk what you are hearing. Your words might be affected by what you are hearing; the moment you hear what will affect your faith, run away for you will never speak right. Your words are there for you to eat and to enjoy.

Any word around you can affect your ear that you may talk what is wrong.

If you hear God you will talk like God. What is disturbing your breakthrough is the doubt you have been told.

This is the new dawn; Good Morning, the day is rising, your victory has come to your life.

Whatever you hear may either affect your faith negatively or positively.

Faith comes by hearing therefore whatever you hear may either affect your faith negatively or positively.

As you hear from above, the devil will bring nonsense; carry on talking the results of God. The Bible instructs us to mediate the word of God day and night.

You must talk what you meditate and your words shall prosper. Prosperity is not in your certificate or what people are saying, it is in the word of God. If you want to prosper, the word of God will take you far.

Many people have a Bible but not the word of God. If you pray a prayer without the word of God, your prayer will be useless.

You need to keep the word of God. When you speak things they shall come to pass and you will witness them.

"³⁴You brood of vipers, how can you who are evil say anything good? For out of the overflow of the heart the mouth speaks.

³⁵ Good people bring good things out of the good stored up in them, and evil people bring evil things out of the evil stored up in them.

³⁶ But I tell you that people will have to give account on the day of judgment for every empty word they have spoken.

³⁷ For by your words you will be acquitted and by your words you will be condemned." **Matthew 12:34-37** *(TNIV)*

This is to show you that you are the way you because of what you have spoken - Be careful on whatever you say.

"¹ Therefore, there is now no condemnation for those who are in Christ Jesus," **Romans 8:1** *(TNIV)*

You don't have any limit when you are with Christ because you are built with Him. There's condemnation to those who speak idle words. When you are with Christ you cannot just speak, you speak what you need to speak.

"²⁴ Anyone who does not love me will not obey my teaching. These words you hear are not my own; they belong to the Father who sent me" **John 14:24** *(TNIV)*

"¹⁷ Sanctify them by the truth; your word is truth." **John 17:17** *(TNIV)*

When you speak the words of Jesus you are set aside, His words are there for an assignment. God wants to give you an assignment, but you don't have words which set you aside. Many of you are supposed to build a mall, but there is no word which is there to set you aside to bring the money of building from the word.

If you are born to lead, why are you behind? I want someone who cannot walk to say *"I will rise up and walk.* Many miracles that Jesus performed were by His spoken words and not from the laying of His hands.

We need to use our words; if I take water and use words to anoint the water, the water will be anointed. Jesus spat on the ground and spoke a word to a blind man.

"Go and wash your eyes" and when the blind man went to wash his eyes, he came back with his eyesight restored. It was not the speckle that healed him, it was the words of Jesus Christ.

The issue of the speckle was not important but the words that followed were important. You are above any situation you may encounter.

Don't fear what you are facing; God's word will never pass away but it shall come to pass. Let them overtake you, but you are the first, when they are busy fighting you, don't fight them because you are the first.

"Jehova you are my refugee and my shelter, whoever fights me fights you"

When David was in war, He said "*Jehovah you are my refugee and my shelter, whoever fights me fights you*". No one has ever defeated David because of the words he spoke. David said God leads him in greener pastures; take the word from above and you shall be lead to greener pastures.

Whatever you are facing, carry on and don't mind what people are saying. Don't be taken by attention by what you are seeing. No on can remove you where God is taking you. When Paul spoke with Timothy, he said Timothy mustn't forget the prophecies given upon his life for they would come to pass. Those prophecies upon your life must lead you to move forward and take you to where they shall be fulfilled.

DOING GOD'S WILL

It' won't be according to your own ability but God's ability.

"23 That was why his parents said, "He is of age; ask him." 24 A second time they summoned the man who had been blind. "Give glory to God and tell the truth," they said. "We know this man is a sinner." 25 He replied, "Whether he is a sinner or not, I don't know. One thing I do know. I was blind but now I see!" 26 Then they asked him, "What did he do to you? How did he open your eyes?" 27 He answered, "I have told you already and you did not listen. Why do you want to hear it again? Do you want to become his disciples too?" 30 The man answered, "Now that is remarkable! You don't know where he comes from, yet he opened my eyes. 31 We know that God does not listen to sinners. He listens to the godly person who does his will." **John 9:23-27, 30-31** *(TNIV)*

The last verse shows that when we do the will of God, when we speak He hears us. In verse 23 you will realise that what Jesus had done was plain but these people (Pharisees) did not know the secret of doing it. Doing God's will is a secret of being heard by God. This man said that God can't listen to a sinner. If God is doing a miracle, it means that you are heard by Him because of you doing His Will. The difference of you hearing God and the one who is not hearing God is that you will be doing God's Will and the one not heard will be doing his own will.

"15 Be very careful, then, how you live—not as unwise but as wise, 16 making the most of every opportunity, because the days are evil. 17 Therefore do not be foolish, but understand what the Lord's will is." **Ephesians 5:15-17** *(TNIV)*

We need to watch our conduct; if the Will of God in our lives does not change us, that Will is questionable. You have been given chance of doing the Will of God and you must not misuse it. Everyone on earth has been given an equal chance of doing the Will of God irrespective of age. As long as you are living on earth you are required to do what God wants you to do; we need to know the Will of God in our lives. We cannot say we are doing His Will not knowing what it is. The Will of God tells us to hear Him. To hear God brings us to obedience. It makes us to be righteous before Him. Many think God can do things without checking our character.

²¹"Not everyone who says to me, 'Lord, Lord,' will enter the kingdom of heaven, but only those who do the will of my Father who is in heaven. ²² Many will say to me on that day, 'Lord, Lord, did we not prophesy in your name and in your name drive out demons and in your name perform many miracles?' ²³ Then I will tell them plainly, 'I never knew you. Away from me, you evildoers!" **Matthew 7:21-23** *(TNIV)*

You can call yourself what you wish to call yourself but if God is not on your side because of you not doing His Will, you are wasting your time. Doing His Will is to stand right with God, to know Him and be one with Him but you will also be tested. Doing God's Will challenges you to be where God is. If you are where God is, then storms will come, winds will come, poverty will come and shame will also come; they are there to question if you are genuine on what you are doing. Not all things are fine until God says is fine.

Doing God's Will is a challenge to Satan himself and this will cause him to also challenge you. Many are facing tribulations doing God's Will but remember that the Bible says that we are more than conquers. Whatever you are facing is not permanent.

I love Christianity because although you may suffer initially, you are guaranteed to be the one to laugh last. Doing God's Will may seem like you are wasting your time but actually it preserves you for a moment, that when you come out, everyone will rejoice about you. When God preserves you, He does it so that you must not see things which are not supposed to see.

"⁴¹ He withdrew about a stone's throw beyond them, knelt down and prayed, ⁴²"Father, if you are willing, take this cup from me; yet not my will, but yours be done." ⁴³ An angel from heaven appeared to him and strengthened him. ⁴⁴ And being in anguish, he prayed more earnestly, and his sweat was like drops of blood falling to the ground." **Luke 22:41-44** *(TNIV)*

How many times have you prayed in agony? Out of what you are facing you are the only one who will come out. Jesus endured the shame because of the glory that was set before Him. Many of you are going through difficulties but believe that it is the Will of God for you. When people are looking at what you are going through, they think God has forsaken you; matter of fact, He is hiding you. Doing God's Will is not easy. It is God's Will to take you to a place were He has ordained you to be.

Sometimes God will allow the worst to happen to you for the best.

Do God's Will!

Many Christians think doing God's Will is when you hear Him telling you to pray for someone, even suffering is part of God's Will for you. It is God who will raise your voice when other voices are fading. Never ever run away fro God, we must always concentrate and do what He is telling us to do. You must carry on and you will see a door leading you out of your troubles. If you are called for God's Will, you will face calamities which will be hard for you. You will even question why things are running smooth for other people whilst they are rough in your life; God wants to show Satan that he is a lair.

Don't be desperate. You have been preserved for a while. When it is God's Will, people cannot define you and they cannot even understand what is going on with you.

13 years ago Apostle has been preaching, Christians laughing at him and he physically saw them leaving his church. I began to enjoy doing God's Will though it was tough in the beginning.

People thought I was desperate, I carried on and began to feel joy and began to preach with joy, I saw them leaving my church one by one, and many have come and even today they are coming.

When you are enjoying God's Will, you will enjoy a life of testimonies. You can't stop the one who has been ordered to do God's Will.

Whatever you do, you will rejoice because you will be doing God's Will. When Stephen (see **Acts 7:54-60**) was being stoned, he never looked at them nor question their cruel persecution towards him, the Bible says that he looked up and saw heaven opened. They were busy with his flesh but he was having a vision. They are busy with you but you are looking at your destiny. They might say you will die but in your vision you are hundred percent well.

Enjoy doing what God says you must do. Those who said you will never work; they themselves will loose their jobs and never work. Some people think you won't make it as if they are your god; there is no one who will remain small when they do God's will.

FIGHT THE GOOD FIGHT OF FAITH

"¹ Praise be to the LORD my Rock, who trains my hands for war, my fingers for battle." **Psalm 144:1** (TNIV)

Where we have read we see David who was always fighting; we see him as a conqueror.

You will realise how possible it was for God to teach David how to fight. If God didn't want us to fight, He wouldn't have taught David how to fight. Our life is a life of wrestling. A Christian's life is a life of wrestling and unless you fight you are telling yourself you are defeated. What is it that you are wrestling with?

Wrestling is a matter of fighting where you either push or hold.

"¹² Fight the good fight of the faith. Take hold of the eternal life to which you were called when you made your good confession in the presence of many witnesses." **1 Timothy 6:12** (TNIV)

We find Timothy speaking about a good fight of faith, meaning there is a fight but our fight is based on pushing and holding. As you are holding, someone wants to take what you are having. Somebody can take things out of your hands if you don't realise what you have so you need to come closer to God. We are in a battle ground. You need to be very serious with what God has entrusted you with otherwise you will be pushed out of your position. What are you holding?

"¹² For our struggle is not against flesh and blood, but against the rulers, against the authorities, against the powers of this dark world and against the spiritual forces of evil in the heavenly realms." **Ephesians 6:12** (TNIV)

The Bible talks about fighting but this is a spiritual one; it is still a fight of faith, a fight against spirits. You are not to take any situation for granted for it might be controlled by principalities. When Jesus sent the Apostles to go and preach the gospel and after preaching Satan fell meaning that he was above.

Any negative force might be controlled somewhere so don't take anything for granted. There is a fight to fight but God will teach you how to fight so that you will overcome your enemies.

Many of you have been pushed or have left what you were holding because of the character of someone controlled by the spirit of Satan. When you see your enemies physically persecuting you, know that they are not your enemies; they are controlled by something but He who leads you will make sure you overcome. Any behaviour is controlled somewhere.

After you have overcome you will stand and the enemy will fall; this is wrestling. If your enemy is standing this might be telling you that you are defeated and you must wrestle. You overcome a good fight of faith by the word of God i.e. you wrestle by the word of God. Faith comes by the word of God taking you to your destiny.

Don't be stagnant; don't undermine yourself, lift your head high and look towards where you are going. Don't look at what people are saying but where God is taking you. Do you have faith? When Satan brings sickness, poverty and all other troubles in your life whilst you have faith derived from the word of God, then you are wrestling.

You will understand that your situation is not permanent. The one who supplies your heart desires is the one teaching you how to fight. You will be more than the conqueror.

"38 Therefore, in the present case I advise you: Leave these men alone! Let them go! For if their purpose or activity is of human origin, it will fail. 39 But if it is from God, you will not be able to stop these men; you will only find yourselves fighting against God." **Acts 5:38-39** *(TNIV)*

When you try to move with God, there are people who analyse you. When the Apostles where moving with God they were analysed. They spoke about Judas who came and gathered people and was killed causing all his followers to be scattered (see Acts 5:37).

The moment you seem to be in a position of leadership, you are analysed and put in a group your annalist understand. They want to put you in a level where they can deal with you and if you overcome, they realise they are fighting God.

God will teach you to fight; you will answer when it is necessary, you will move when you are directed. Others could not reach your level so they try to put you on a level where they have stopped others. It is only a sign from heaven that silences your opposers. He who fights you when you are fighting is fighting God.

There are people who think when they fight you they are doing it on you but they don't know your battle teaches you how to wrestle. God teaches you to move, to sit, to fight and to answer today he who fights you will meet your Father.

Your family treats you somehow because they have never seen anyone like you. Your fingers have power to bring what you want. You can fight when you are asleep. You need to reach a level where you have to be like Christ.

There are people who say there is no God in front of you; they don't know that he is behind you and pushing you. When you are busy wrestling, your competitors are looking at you physically but they can't see you spiritually and they can't see the One who is pushing you.

Like David, you will use just one stone to put the devil down in the name of Jesus. You don't need to push the wall of Jericho with your hands. When you are singing and praising the Living God, you will push down the wall of Jericho.

You thought you were pushing alone, you were not alone.

"²⁴ So Jacob was left alone, and a man wrestled with him till daybreak. ²⁵ When the man saw that he could not overpower him, he touched the socket of Jacob's hip so that his hip was wrenched as he wrestled with the man." **Genesis 32:24-25** (TNIV)

When Jacob was wrestling, he was wrestling to change his name. God gave him favour but could not allow him to go back to Israel with the same name otherwise he would be known as a robber. Abraham realised that it was not just a wrestle but a blessing. There are wrestles which are there to defeat you.

What you are going through is a blessing in disguise. The Bible says when Jacob was fighting the Angel; the Angel touched Jacob and gave him a sign. No one will fight you because God is making you suitable for your blessings. God can't bring you this far to leave you. There are afflictions that have come in your life but God will teach you to fight and all of them will bow.

God is making you abnormal - When you see an abnormal car, you make sure you have to get out of the way. Though Isaac was initially being fought when he was digging up wells, he fought until he was given space and named that place, Rehoboth (see Genesis 26:18-22).

CONFIDENCE

We all know that Jesus died for us and went to the cross because of the love he had for all of us. He loved all of us, He saw what would happen if He hadn't agreed. No one could agree to die in the manner Jesus died in. Jesus preferred to die as a sinner that we can live a righteous life. Many of us are lacking to understand that Jesus died because He loved and still loves us.

*"31 What, then, shall we say in response to these things? If God is for us, who can be against us? 32 He who did not spare his own Son, but gave him up for us all—how will he not also, along with him, graciously give us all things? **Romans 8:31-32** (TNIV)*

Jesus loved us to an extent that He wanted us to have all things. Do you know that there is nothing difficult for the Lord? We need confidence!

I was asking myself how David approached Goliath; it was not easy as we think. David had confidence in the Lord - We are lacking confidence. This is the meaning of confidence: it is a conviction or a belief that you maintain until the end understanding that the Lord will help you. The moment you confess the name of Jesus, you need to have confidence.

We are lacking confidence. The battles we meet take away our confidence or they affect our trust in the Lord for you cannot put confidence in the one you don't trust. You prayed and when you didn't see results you questioned if God was with you.

When we set time for ourselves to get results, we always get disappointments and that's how our faith diminishes. The reason why we have strategies is because we are lacking to trust in His name, we don't have confidence in the Lord. He who has confidence in the Lord, in him there is no time; he will totally depend only onto the Lord. He believes that though there is nothing visible, the blessing will still come to his hand.

When you have confidence, you don't worry about who is better than you; you can't compete. The moment you don't see results you don't worry. The confidence in you will rise up. The more you don't get what you want is the more your confidence is sharpened; it becomes brighter, stronger and more visible.

If your confidence is not challenged it might be telling you that it has gone down and your trust in the Lord is broken. This leads to your faith being inactive and if it is inactive our actions cannot please God therefore you will not be able to pray, read the word of God or even fast; you will be limited.

Many of you the challenges you face are not there to stop you but rather to challenge your confidence. The challenges are there to tell you to plan better, to move forward and to gain more confidence. You need to trust God; by doing that the more it gets tough, you move forward making it impossible for any situation to stop you.

Shadrach, Meshach and Abednego couldn't bow down before King Nebuchadnezzar (see **Daniel 3:6-25**). God made them to have life in a furnace and their God was worshiped. You can still breathe where no one can breathe.

The Importance of Confidence:

"Confident of your obedience, I write to you, knowing that you will do even more than I ask." "[21] **1. Philemon 1:21** (TNIV)

Confidence makes you to do more. The difference between you and your enemy; it's your ability to do more. The reason why your enemy will fight you is because you are better than your enemy as you can do more than your enemy. Can you see why you are facing trouble? Satan does not what to rest as he knows you can do more.

Jesus said He had come to give us life, not only life but more (see **John 10:10**).

You must maintain your confidence. Many people want to die now; their confidence has been buried; when confidence is no more, hope has left. When you don't have confidence you don't have hope and if you don't have hope you don't have faith therefore you can't please God and you will go to hell.

There are people looking at you thinking that you will fail. You can do more. Stop crying.

"³⁵ So do not throw away your confidence; it will be richly rewarded. ³⁶ You need to persevere so that when you have done the will of God, you will receive what he has promised." **2. Hebrews 10:35-36** (TNIV)

Confidence brings a reward.

"⁶ And without faith it is impossible to please God, because anyone who comes to him must believe that he exists and that he rewards those who earnestly seek him." **Hebrews 11:6** (TNIV)

When you come to God believing in Him, there is a reward. Whatever you have went through; crush them by establishing confidence in the Lord.

A wife who doesn't have confidence will always check whether the husband comes home in time or not. Many times because of time, we develop suspicions and this is derived from lacking confidence. Get out of time and get unto Jesus Christ.

"¹⁴ We have come to share in Christ, if indeed we hold firmly till the end our original conviction." **Hebrews 3:14** (TNIV)

When we receive Jesus, many things come to remove us from what we initially believe in. We are partakers, one with Christ. Christ doesn't want us to be like Him before He went to the cross, He wants us to be like Him after the resurrection; a life of the impossibilities.

One day the disciples were afraid locking themselves in a room. Jesus came and went through the wall. There was no wall that could stop Him. If we can be one with Jesus after He resurrected, we can do strange things. When Jesus wants to bless you, He changes your complexion, your attire, how you walk and how you talk.

Writer's Prayer.

My Father my creator, arise within me, enrich and empower me with your gifts.
My Father, my saviour please touch my life and change my name. Renew the right spirit in
me my Lord and make me the woman of virtue and excellence. Let me have the courage
to write the things that will change the mind set of evil doers to believe in Christianity.
I pray for every power that is holding me from reaching my destiny, every power that
has stolen my star and steal my position to be loose right now in Jesus mighty name.
Father I cover all my works with the blood of Jesus and whoever
read my books will be blessed abundantly.
Let every evil power manipulating my anointing be destroyed by fire in Jesus name.
Amen. Amen and Amen.